THE HARD BOARDS BITE INTO MY BODY

THE HARD BOARDS BITE INTO MY BODY

Poems about Politics and Power

Jack Howard

Cover by Sally Alexandre

ARTHUR H. STOCKWELL LTD
Torrs Park, Ilfracombe, Devon, EX34 8BA
Established 1898
www.ahstockwell.co.uk

© Jack Howard, 2021
First published in Great Britain, 2021

The moral rights of the author have been asserted.

All rights reserved.
No part of this publication may be reproduced
or transmitted in any form or by any means,
electronic or mechanical, including photocopy,
recording, or any information storage and
retrieval system, without permission
in writing from the copyright holder.

British Library Cataloguing-in-Publication Data.
A catalogue record for this book is available
from the British Library.

ISBN 978-0-7223-5099-7
Printed in Great Britain by
Arthur H. Stockwell Ltd
Torrs Park   Ilfracombe
Devon   EX34 8BA

ACKNOWLEDGEMENTS

I would like to thank Sally Alexandre, without whom this volume would not have got off the ground.

I would also like to thank Namirla Bankhead for her continued patience, the Inkspirations writers' group for their support, and any other persons, too numerous to mention, who have helped me on this journey.

CONTENTS

Politics	9
The Intelligence of Politics	10
Silence	11
Scorched Earth	12
Saddam	14
Equality	15
Listen	16
Harry Kay	17
Ritual	18
The Price of War	20
Gail Is Dead	21
Back to Basics	22
Remembrance Sunday	24
Outcasts	25
I Lie with Ghosts	26
Justice	28
Freedom	30
The Wall	31
Normandy	32
No Longer Needed	34
Cardboard City	36
A Battlefield Stained Red	39
Duet	40
Who Is the Terrorist	42
Promises	43
Politics 2	44
The Twisted Truth	45
Abuse	46
Freedom	47
Glory	48
Silence 2	49
The Hard Boards	50
Karmen Rouge	52
Little Children	53

War	54
Mass Destruction	56
Greed	57
Rape	58
Survival	60
Tears	62
Politics 3	64
Aleppo	65
Just Another Bum	66
Politics 4	68
The General's War	69
Poverty	70
Telegram	71
Yet Another Domestic	72
Cameron's Prayer	73
Heroes	74
Christmas	75
Penny for the Guy	76
The Hanging Tree	77
The Beast Is Always There	78
A Death Untold	81
Politics 5	82
Equality	83
Political Ideology	84
Poverty 2	85
Ashes to Ashes	86

POLITICS

he dictated his speech to his secretary
as he waited for his lunch to arrive
when he had finished dictating
he had her read it back to him

he smiled to himself as the first course was served
the courses came and went
as did the wine and the champagne
when he had finished
he phoned his secretary
to remind her to end his speech
with 'we are all in it together'

on the way home he stopped the car
outside a fish and chip shop
(he had already alerted his PR
to make sure that the press were there)
he ordered a fish supper
making sure he was recognised

when he got home he gave
the fish supper to his dog
telling it that these were difficult times
so it had better not leave anything

he went to bed
with an air of satisfaction
politics is a good game
as long as you are on top and
you don't take it too seriously

THE INTELLIGENCE OF POLITICS

an IQ of 140
divided by three score years and ten
equals 2
two bits of intelligence per year

must be about average
for a politician

SILENCE

the guns fall silent
once again
and in the evening
the evening of my mind
I can hear the sounds
that should have been
that were

birds singing
children laughing

but
in the silence
left by the guns
there is nothing
only
the silence

until tomorrow

SCORCHED EARTH

and
there was a time
when the earth
was divided
into four nations
one for each compass point

and
everyone was happy
and
all was at peace

but
one sub-tribe
moved across the
longitudinal line
because the grass
was greener

and
one sub-tribe
moved across
the equator
because the ore
was richer
and so they went to war

one hundred
years later
there were no
sub-tribes
there was no
green grass
there was no ore

and
God said
there will be
no more humans
and the devil laughed

SADDAM

Saddam
is a man
or so we hear
or maybe
he is
a puppeteer

pulling the strings
the strings of war
killing people
for evermore

Saddam
is a man
or so we hear

EQUALITY?

How is it that the salt of the earth
when fighting for their right to work
become the scum of the earth

how is it that politicians
elected on their socialist principles
take graft and send their kids to public schools

How is it that the government
introduces laws against discrimination
and then imprisons more blacks than whites

How is it that women have equal rights
and yet are less than men
are battered by men
are raped by men

How is it that in the age of children's rights
they are still abused
they are still murdered

How is that in the age of enlightenment
love does not seem to play a part

How is it
I don't know

LISTEN

how many have sat
watching over the valley
waiting for them to return
listening for the signal

how many hands
so long ago
leant on this stone
soaked the same sun
sought the same shade

how many stayed
behind the walls
fearing the battle
the cries the screams

how many waited
for their hearts to die
how many victories
were worth the cost

how many stood silent
until the burning gate
pushed open wide
sealed their fates
ended their lives

and now who stands
on the piles of rubble
on all that's left

who sits and listens
to the curlew's cry
to the jackdaw's scream
and then who says to me
there is no tale to tell

HARRY KAY

Harry Kay
lived in a day
his life

each day the same
each night oblivion

Harry Kay
with money
bought cider
bought friends
bought death

a park bench
his deathbed

dirty
unshaven
unwanted

Harry Kay
did not live
his life that day

RITUAL

he lay
not moving lest
some had stayed back
before him lay his wife
in her lifeblood
her only release
her death

the blood had ceased to flow
the young screams had faded
long ago as they were bound
and carried off

the old lay dead around him

he slowly stood his gaze
fixed on the carnage
too much for tears
too much for rage

the smouldering huts
crashed to their deaths
midst clouds of sparks

the others now so far away
would come to this
all smiles and cries
and hunting tales to tell

but when they came
no cries of joy
would fill the night
only the stench
of burning flesh
and the light
of funeral pyres

and then
their rituals performed
their weapons sharp
they would pursue
unto their deaths

but they would see
their loved ones
once again even if
with dying eyes

he stood and waited
bloodied and weak
but proud to have fought

he gazed gently down
to his wife
and closed her eyes
that no longer saw
and kissed her lips
that no longer felt

THE PRICE OF WAR

if Bosnia was in China
would the UN be there

if Kuwait had no oil
would we be there

if the Falklands had not been strategic
if Gibraltar was in the North Sea
if Hitler had invaded Japan

our morality
it seems
rests in our wallets

GAIL IS DEAD

there are no flowers on her grave
not in a crematorium
only dust

she has not gone from me
images pass through my mind
of deflowered youth
hardly budded
now gone

memory of her lives on
through a thousand Gails
or more
red-rimmed eyes
hardened mouths
scarred bodies
burnt-out souls

they live and die like Gail

BACK TO BASICS

are you going to bed in a real bed
tonight John Major
are you going home to a real house
or to a cardboard box
will you bathe in a real bathroom

I suppose you are all right
I mean
if you lose your job
you will not lose you salary
and there will be plenty more jobs
your city friends will see to that

you won't have to do
a boring work experience
you won't have to be
a cheap tea boy
you won't have to be abused
so as to keep your job

you won't be sleeping
in a hostel
beds crammed together
smelling all the others

go to your parties
John Major
drink your champagne
sleep in your freshly laundered sheets
in your centrally heated room

and while you sleep
dream about your back-to-basics policy
about having a home
about having a job
about having self-respect

dream on John Major
dream yourself into oblivion
for that is where you belong

REMEMBRANCE SUNDAY

and when the
dust dies down
and the bullets
cease their whine
of instant death

we lie in silence

and we remember
those we have
left behind

and sometimes
even smile

but then
the whistle blows
its shrill blast
cutting through our
thoughts and
shattering
our dreams

and the next
time there is
silence there
are new faces
next to mine

and I wonder
how long it will
be before there
is a new face
where mine is

OUTCASTS

the homeless the addicts
the failures the lost
the tramps the thieves the robbers
the fallen

the ones we pass and ignore
about whom we do not care
we judge and then we punish

we try to treat them fairly
but we do not succeed

the antisocial outcasts
society's doormats

but
they are not as good as us
they are not as clean
as honest
as caring
as responsible
as holy

I wonder
who will get to heaven first

I LIE WITH GHOSTS

I heard the screams
before I saw
I felt the blows
the force they bore
I saw the blood
the queen of red
and your last breath
and then your death

I stood and watched
but nothing did I
do to stop the pain
I stood and watched
your lifeblood drain

and when they asked
I told no lie
my orders were
simply to obey
but how could you
stand back and stare
at the torment
meted out there

I closed my eyes
in my defence
I did not see
the coup de grâce
it was my duty
to God and king
I could not see
what this would bring

I now lie down
with ghosts each night
but you don't want
to hear my plight

you were not there
I stopped mid breath
their eyes upon me
spoke of death

I whispered low
you were not there
how could you know
the cross I bear

their sentence passed
I hung my head
and braved myself
to join my dead

JUSTICE

I sat and watched your husband
as he was sentenced by the judge
he will lose five years of his life
but he may come back sooner
on parole

in the meantime we will help
we will guide you through the
difficulties which will confront you
now that you have no husband
so to speak of
now that your children have no father

we will try to alleviate your worries
we will comfort you when we have time
we will make the loss of your husband
a little easier to bear

you are not entirely alone
as we have your name on a file
you can see us whenever you want to
providing that we are here
and we will see you even though we
are understaffed and overworked

you see when anyone is sent to prison
when anyone loses slices of their life
when wives are lonely and children fatherless
we are here to help you and
in so doing to salve the conscience of
society

I know he may be mentally ill
I know his personality may be disturbed
he may not have had a chance
his parents separated he unloved
but we will try to rehabilitate him on release
now dry your tears my dear
and in the meantime
here is my card. . . .

FREEDOM

they stood
upon the ramparts
eyes alight hearts proud
the eagle-topped standards
disappearing over the hill
never to be seen again

holding tight upon each other
and upon their new-found freedom
they watched each other's eyes
in the cold morning light
smoke curling to the sunrise

they stood
not knowing what to do
except perhaps
to close the gate

THE WALL

the barbed wire lying
in wait
on top of the wall
told its story well

waiting for the next
would-be escapee
its razor-sharp teeth
hoping to draw blood

an innocent life
wasted
trying to escape
to freedom

the irony is freedom
and dying for it
is no longer an issue
on either side of the wall
since the wall came down

NORMANDY

the dead haunt me
as I stand among
the ordered lines
of the crosses
covering the disordered
bodies of the dead

their screams still echo
above the noise of battle

straight lines
all white
all clean
all gleaming

their screams still echo
above the sounds of battle

on the cross
it gives the name
it gives the age
it gives the rank
it gives the regiment

it does not say
in which ditch they lay
how many pieces were
torn from their body
how long it took them to die

it does not tell of their prayers
or of their despair
their relief at oblivion

but their screams still echo
above the din of battle

did they think of king and country
did they revel in their glorious death
obeying orders for honour
or fear of being shot

just their name
their age
their rank
their regiment

NO LONGER NEEDED

his voice cut through her
like a razor blade
opening her heart
laying it bare

I am leaving
he said

she was torn
her anger rising
but despair
also competing

she cried as
she felt the knife
plunge deeper
twisting and turning

when
she whispered
why
she whispered

now
he said
stonily
coldly

why
because I no longer need you

she stood
absolutely still
frozen

need
he had said
need

what about love
she realised
he did not love her

she had felt that before
but she had not listened

to its whispered pleas
ignored
repressed
rejected

but now it was here
stark
in white light

no longer needed
no longer wanted

she bowed her head
tears flowing down her cheeks
running round the curve of her mouth
dripping from her chin

she wept silently
as he walked away

CARDBOARD CITY

they sat in the darkness
hungry
tired

what will happen to us
she said softly huskily
quietly

I don't know
he shouted
loudly aggressively
defensively

I don't fucking know

there was a silence
an agony
a bond
which made each other reach out

broken fingernails touched
dirty hands clasped

the cardboard melted in the rain
their love for each other
now colder than an Arctic storm
was once a Sahara heat

but not now
not here
too hungry
too sad

I'm hungry she said
she was dying

He knew she was dying
but did not want to know
he did not want to be part of her dying
he only wanted to be part of her living

he could not face the hurt
he had enough hurt of his own

she had known for a long time
an eternity it seemed that she was dying
but she did not want him to know
she knew that he had enough pain
she did not want to give him more
she did not want to see him hurt
she did not want to die seeing his hurt

She crawled deeper into the dampness
and coldness of her blankets
deeper into the melting cardboard
away from the wind that made her cough

he went out

he wanted to stay
he could love her alive
but he did not know how to love her death
only how to love her life

never is a long time
never is forever
he stood in the rain

she waited for death

he waited for her death
standing by the river
a place they had found
so many years ago
or was it days

a place under the trees
where they had first made love
where hearts
had first entwined
tenderly carefully of each other
and lovingly touching

he shook his head
to clear the memories of what was
of what could have been
of what was

she lay
limbs stiff
lips blue
death softening her face
smoothing away the lines
of her living

he looked at her
and wished he could join her
in the infinity
of death
of her death
and his death

A BATTLEFIELD STAINED

from bloodied field
I write these words
with gun in hand
and agonies shared
a battlefield stained red
with those about to die
and those already dead

they sacrificed themselves
for those they love
their death o'ershadowed
by fierce debate
which for decades
will not abate
as the awesome noise
crescendos to a din
too awful to imagine

and
as the fruitless killing
goes on in numbers far
beyond our comprehension

the politician hiding
in his safe retreat
plays chess with those
we are hoping to defeat

and sits in warmth
and safely fed
pontificates about the dead

DUET

and the bombs fell
earth shattering

your golden hair

and the din grew
louder bursting my ears

caressing your shoulders

a crescendo of screams
the rape of innocents

trailing down to the curve

the hiss of shrapnel
from exploding shells

of your breasts and beyond

the bullets clattering
off the pockmarked
concrete walls

your eyes reflecting the sky
their blueness never ending

sounds reverberating

the redness of your lips

the blood running
over pavements
diluted by the rain

so soft so tender

the rattle of machine
guns drowning the
screams of children
and as we kiss

and as we kiss

I feel your life force
flow from your body

I feel your life force
flow through my body

WHO IS THE TERRORIST

he is a terrorist
he kills innocent people

but your president did
in Hiroshima

but that was different

how

that's not the point

that is the point

terrorists blow up women
and children

presidents blow up women
and children

but they placed a bomb
where they knew children
would be

but they dropped a bomb
where they knew children
would be

we can't have
terrorists like that

we can't have
presidents like that

you're talking crap

am I

PROMISES

bruised face cut lips
a broken nose
a loveliness injured

how many times
a never-again promise
broken
the following night

a dream ruptured
an entity crushed
a slave cowering
in the corner

bruised face cut lips
waiting for the next time

POLITICS 2

at the end of his
speech
he burped and fell
over
the press office said
a mild stroke

his wife said she was
leaving him as she
could no longer stand
the four or five strokes
per week

his mistress
shrugged her shoulders
in complete boredom

he was cheered out
of hospital and named
victim of the year

next year
predictably
he was
re-elected

THE TWISTED TRUTH

and
the weapons roll off
the European
assembly lines
whilst other countries
are banned
from manufacturing
similar weapons

I wonder
what would happen
if the UN inspectors
inspected Portman Down
or
other European sites
would they ban them
from production

I think not

ABUSE

suddenly truthed
yes truthed

the blue raised bump
on your forehead
was real
was no accident

the tears in your eyes
were wet
your despair
your anguish
became mine

but
what could I offer
on a cold October night
snow in the air
you're his child asleep

how could I tell you
that the love
so strong in youth
would change in time

the violence
the beatings
the humiliations

can that be love

I cannot stand your fear
I cannot stand your fear

FREEDOM

Sergei Prokofiev
wrote a symphony
Karl Marx
wrote a thesis

they both believed
in freedom
one through music
one through economics

but neither attained it

and today
more than a
century later
the workers
(and the non-workers)
hope for the same

but it is too late
or is it

GLORY

when you lay there
flesh bullet-torn
bones broken
did you think of
glory and of England

or did you think of
home where lay
your wife and son
and a letter
not yet finished and
never to be read

a love song
written in tears

when you lay there
did you think of glory
or did you think of home

SILENCE 2

little girl silent
don't you dare cry
no one will hurt you
as long as you lie
silent

little girl silent
eyes wide and deep
no one will blame you
as long as you keep
silent

little girl silent
inside all pain
do as I tell you and
make sure you remain
silent

little girl silent
go on your way
you may get a present
as long as you stay

silent

THE HARD BOARDS

the hard boards
bite into my body
the guttural shouts
hurt my ears
the screams of
the women wound
my soul

but
today I live
and there is hope
and maybe
and maybe
there is release

and
yet as I eat my soup
so thin
I think that I am alive

I work until
I fall
I work until
I cannot work

and
then I sleep
and in my sleep
I dream of you

I dream of our
house and garden
I dream of you
walking into
my arms
I dream
of you

there are rumours of
experiments with people
but they are rumours

there are rumours of
extermination and death
but I am alive

there are rumours of
rape and torture of my love
which I can't accept

even now when I see the ovens
when I see the piles of clothes
the belongings of my family
I can't accept
and never will

the hard boards
bite into my body

KARMEN ROUGE

in retrospect
a mistake was made
that is now costing us
political credibility

it should not have happened
but then war nowadays
does tend to be total
and Cambodia is far away
it has no oil or gold
so it was not a priority

it was an error of judgment
and it has cost the party dearly
but we will be back
we will bury our past
as they bury their dead
and forget the killing fields
still stained blood red

LITTLE CHILDREN

little children
singing shouting
playing ball
playing tig

little children
shouting laughing
falling tumbling
acting big

little children
screaming bleeding
hacked to pieces
on their bed

little children
falling tumbling
lying still
not playing dead

WAR

we had been praying
and reading the Bible
I sensed the tension
but I was too young
to know why
and was sent to bed

the hammering on the door
woke me suddenly
I heard the voices
loud guttural aggressive
I crept under my bed
taking teddy with me

I could hear Mama crying
I could hear Papa pleading
and the sounds of kicking
and stamping and people
falling

I heard loud footsteps
on the stairs and
I shrank back to
the far corner of
my bed hiding place

I heard Papa saying that
I was staying with relatives
they were all over the room
I saw their leather boots
go back and forth past my bed

I heard Mama scream
and felt the bed groan
as if many people were
jumping up and down

I heard the gunshot
and saw Papa fall on
the floor blood spurting
from his head
Mama screamed

and then the sounds
of the men leaving
I bit my fist and waited
tears stinging my eyes

after a while I crept
from my hiding place
Papa and Mama
did not move

I did not know what to do
I went around the house
I found a hammer
and some nails and
nailed the door closed

I sat and prayed that
they would never
visit again

MASS DESTRUCTION

and as the allies
search for weapons
of mass destruction
they roll off the conveyor
belts in England and in
America protected by
the pretentious belief
that they will never be used

remember Hiroshima
remember Nagasaki

if you don't
they do

GREED

and
the big bird landed
to gulp the food

strutting his stuff
like a pop star
at a concert

strutting his stuff

and
the others
looked on in awe
and wished
that they could
strut their stuff

but
the big bird ignored them
and took advantage
of them
and ate more than
his share of their
collective pantry

and strutted his stuff

just like some politicians

RAPE

I saw the rape that night
as 1 looked into your eyes
highlighted by the violence
and blackened by the fires
of hate that burn there still

the same night I stopped dreaming
of green and pleasant lands
and only saw the moonscape
moulded by the bloodied hands
which all had learnt to fear

I saw your eyes freeze over
I heard your final sigh
your skin take whitened pallor
your body there to lie
your eyes wide open staring

that night I saw my death
reflected in your eyes
now sealed forever in fate
before my last goodbyes
and my life to realise

yes I saw the rape that night
and the horror ever since
has haunted all my waking hours
my conscience to convince
that my hand was never raised

and yet if blameless so I be
then who can be at fault
is there anyone who never
has done something they revolt
are we blameless to the end

I saw the rape that night
as I looked into your eyes
highlighted by the violence
and blackened by the fires
of hate that burn there still

SURVIVAL

he awoke to blackness
the small window
neither emitting
nor receiving light

he yawned
it had been a bad night
the bombs falling
shaking the buildings
and the screams

he thanked God
that his house
had a cellar

he went to the toilet
and wondered for how long
would he have water

it had been like this
for many months
and all he could do
was hope and pray
for change

he walked the streets
waiting for the screams
of the rockets and the bombs
and the people
but there was silence

the bodies lay scattered
on the streets
in the gutters
in pools of blood
he no longer retched
he no longer saw them
his only thought was of food
the only emotion
was survival

three days ago
he had stolen bread
from an old woman
six days ago
he had killed a man
who had tried to steal
from him

he wondered when peace
would finally come
when the bombing would stop
when the rattle of machine guns
would cease and then
how would he cope
with the silence
with his enemy
next door

would he still steal
would he still kill
he knew the change
would be hard
but he did not know
how he would react
how he would survive
or whether he would survive

TEARS

and
his army
marched jackbooted
through her mind
trampling over all
her dreams crushing
her hopes and
releasing her fears
until she could
stand no more

but she had no army
she had no weapons

so she cried
hoping that her
tears would wash
away the damage
flush out the
intruders and
leave her clean

his army found
that the rush of
tears bogged
them down
stopping their advance
forcing them to retreat
until they were
swept out to run
haphazardly down
her cheek and
fall off her chin

she felt better and smiled
he felt frustrated and frowned

and
a truce was
declared

at least
for the moment

POLITICS 3

in another life
he postulated forgiveness
in this one he didn't bother
his political career
was above all else

his appearance in church
a good photo shoot
almost as good as the other
one talking to prisoners
and recommending community
sentences – except for the person
who broke into his home
for him he recommended life
(joking of course
or was he)

he supported women's lib
as long as men were in power

he supported the youth
as long as they went elsewhere

he supported every minority
as long as they supported themselves
and didn't claim benefits

he gave talks to the deaf
and showed pictures to the blind

his mistress delighted him
his colleagues in the chamber
always supported him
and praised him as
a good solid member

needless to say
he was re-elected

ALEPPO

the bombs keep dropping
the women keep praying
heads of state gather
and sit round a table
the rhetoric is the same
the same as it has been
for the past millennia

economic sanctions
is the cry even though
this will increase the
death rate of civilians
and plunge women and children
into greater poverty

and still the bombs drop
on hospitals
on schools
accidently of course
collateral damage
says the west
on whom bombs
do not drop

and the heads of state
reconvene their conference
and they argue
and they blame
and as ever
do nothing

JUST ANOTHER BUM

he stood on the corner
leaning against the wall
knowing if he left it
he would fall over

fall over yet again

he peered out
under the brim
of his uncoloured
hat

fuck you all
he said
fuck you all
and swayed
grasping the corner
in a desperate
attempt to stand

he failed

as he fell
his head struck
the brickwork

he lay for two
hours before
anyone thought
something may be wrong

he was dead on arrival

his death did not
make headlines

a pauper's burial
ended his story

no one thought about
his medal for courage
his profession
his family

his true worth
his past record

his charity was
unrecorded

his loyalty
was not mentioned
he was just another bum

rest in peace
if you can

POLITICS 4

Mr Smith questioned his MP
is it right that people in England
live in poverty

poverty is relative
I lived in a council house for two weeks
to see how you did it
and I paid my rent and rates
(from my expenses of course)

did your washer break down
did your kids need school uniforms
did you pay the bloke round the corner
(the one who breaks legs for a living)

I paid my way unlike some

bollocks

people in England do live in poverty
all you need to do is look

THE GENERAL'S WAR

the private asked the general
why they were fighting the war
to protect our king and homeland
was the general's reply

but we have not been invaded
the private mused to the general
but they will and soon said the general
but we are an island said the private
and they do not have a navy

they will have a navy quite soon
and then they will invade us
so we have to be ready to fight
on the beaches or in the streets
the patriotism shining in his eyes

on his bunk that night the private
wrote to his wife and his children
the letter contained only one word
'goodbye'

POVERTY

poverty is relative
so they say

they also say
everyone is equal

they also say
everyone has
all that they need

try telling that
to someone in
a queue for the
food bank or waiting
for a triple
bypass

they may have
a different perception

TELEGRAM

how did you feel
when the telegram came
when with trembling fingers
you read

missing presumed dead

did you collapse
on the chair
tears rolling
down your cheeks

how will you tell his son
his mother
his father

how will you cope

half of you died
that day
on a muddy field
in Flanders

but life goes on
especially for politicians
and for generals

but not for you
it ended
with that
telegram

YET ANOTHER DOMESTIC

the bruises no longer show
at least
not to others
but they remain to you
the pain
the anguish

just another domestic
said the police

he's always canny
said the neighbours

it must be her fault
the cow

CAMERON'S PRAYER

Cameron stood on the balcony
oh pale moon you who can
control the tides
let me have some of your power
so that I can control the tides
of voters who in their ignorance
vote against me

no – amend that
give me all of your power
so that I can control
all of the world so that
they will bend to my will
and to my ideals
so that I will save the world

oh yes
give me your power
give me all of your power

HEROES

the heroes of a century ago
were not the generals
nor the politicians
they were the mothers
who looked after
the next generation

knitting socks for
fathers brothers husbands
worrying every day
dealing with rations
dealing with money
(or the lack of it)
and waiting

waiting for the telegram
and hoping and praying
it would never come

CHRISTMAS

I sit with my turkey dinner
all the trimmings
naturally
plenty of wine
and Christmas pud
celebrating Christmas
or somebody's birthday
(I forgot whose)
vague memories
of church

I watch television adverts
showing starving children
and poor people
so I switch over

why the hell do they
show such misery
at Christmas
when everyone is so merry

if they sterilise all the poor countries
and make the people work
there would be no problem
God I should run this world

would you like
a whisky love
single malt of course
or brandy perhaps
whatever you want

PENNY FOR THE GUY

penny for the guy sir
who is the guy
Nigel Farage sir
here's fifty pounds
thank you sir
will you be here tomorrow
yes sir
see you then

hi Bill hi James
collecting for the guy
who is it this time
Nigel Farage
made much
about two thousand

who is it tomorrow
David Cameron

THE HANGING TREE

The slave owners stood
around the hanging tree
in groups of two or three
laughing and joking with
the preacher

the black women
standing at the back
too frightened to speak
or look at their menfolk
swinging in the breeze

they had tried to escape
from slavery
from beatings

the preacher said a prayer

Lord if they have a soul
forgive them for escaping

the white leader of the men
was watching and listening

hold on there preacher
or people will think that
they are human
just like us

the crowd laughed
the black wives silently wept
and swayed in the breeze
in unison with their menfolk

THE BEAST IS ALWAYS THERE

so Mr Chancellor you have done well
you have kept the rich happy
so they'll vote for you next time
and kept the middle classes
away from revolution
and made the poor poorer
and even more powerless

in the Industrial Revolution
the workers kept the rich
in the luxuries they were
accustomed to whilst
the working class struggled
to feed and clothe themselves

after two world wars things
seemed to get better
especially for the poor
but the beast was
only lurking beneath the surface
in the dark corners
awaiting his chance
to once again take control
to once again take full power
to once again line its pockets
at the expense of the poor

so where is the Labour Party
where are the Liberals
we are deafened by their silence
their hypocrisy takes away our breath

where then is democracy
when a handful of families
control the nation's wealth
when the poor are crippled
by minimum wages

and where is equality
when women earn less
than men
when further education
grants are taken away
when communities are decimated
and set against each other

and whilst the workers drink
cheap coffee and beer
the upper classes wallow in
champagne and eat the best
food whilst congratulating
each other on their successes
forgetting that the waiters
and waitresses are on
minimum wages or less

the rich dressed in their
finery made in the sweat
shops of the East where
the workers are paid
only enough to feed
themselves and their families
(or even less)

So
Mr Conservative Prime Minister
Mr Shadow Chancellor
and all the others
will you sleep tonight

better than those on the streets
better than those in hostels

and when you eat your cooked breakfast
your subsidised meal at the house
spare a thought for those who have nothing
that's if you can spare the time
to think about them

but remember
although you may hide
behind your power

you remain guilty
because of your silence

A DEATH UNTOLD

he lay on the bench
his bed for years
swaddled in
yesterday's news
dreaming of a soft bed
of soft arms holding him
of I-love-you kisses

but they were only dreams
dreams of faraway times
dreams of rejected youth
of unrequited love

everyone knew him
but no one knew his name
or his dreams

one morning
he did not wake
there was no funeral
no mourners
no flowers

POLITICS 5

they sit on their asses
day after day in the House
that's if they attend

they talk about crises
arguing back and forth
but make no decisions

how many people
have to die before
their asses get sore
and they all do nothing

they go back to their castles
back to their country mansions
all well protected
at our expense

conclusions not reached
decisions aborted
as they eat five-course meals
provided by the people

EQUALITY

she lives in a hovel
no hope no money
hardly enough food
for her children

her MP postulates
it's her fault
why should the state pay
the father should pay

everyone is equal
but there are many
who are deceived
abused
coerced

I don't suppose that
there are many MPs
who've had it up against
the wall behind the pub
in a search for affection
or even for the promise
of love

eat your canapes
drink your champagne
keep blaming the poor
the homeless
the unemployed

they fornicate
because they are oversexed
they are lazy and chaotic

that reminds me of
some politicians

POLITICAL IDEOLOGY

the political ideology of today
is based on yesterday's thoughts
and does not reach tomorrow
but shimmers in the ether
of in-between

nothing new is expressed
just a rehash of yesterday
a rhetoric of speeches
not of new actions

and the rich stay rich

and the poor stay poor

POVERTY 2

how can we deny poverty
whilst the soup kitchens are open
how can we deny poverty
and support the food banks

we despise the Eastern rulers
who live in luxury
whilst their subjects
die in the streets

we despise some countries
for seeking out and shooting children

at the same time we
force our elderly citizens
to choose between food or heat
humiliate our unemployed
and single parents

we force single homeless
young and old
to live on the streets
whilst we live in
central-heated houses

long live Western society

ASHES TO ASHES

Oh glorious Houses of Parliament
How still we see thee lie
Beneath the ashes of England
Which came down from the sky

A couple of well-placed hydrogen bombs
From where we do not know
Dropped on to various cities
(they missed out Catfish Row)